JOHN WAYNE

TRUE GRIT

AMERICAN

Published by: Wilma Russell
Compiled by: Wilma Russell
Design & Production by: Elena Ellis
Editor: Jane Pattie
Introduction by Jane Pattie

Web Site: www.TheDukeBook.com

Printed in China • 2010
ISBN 0-9670534-4-7
Library of Congress Control Number: 2006905080

Special thanks to:

Cindy Mitchum, for permission to use a portion of lyrics from the book and CD,
America, Why I Love Her. Lyrics by John Mitchum.

For John Wayne memorabilia please visit: www.johnwaynebirthplace.org

John Wayne Cancer Institute: www.jwci.org

I PLEDGE ALLEGIANCE

JOHN WAYNE

TRUE GRIT

AMERICAN

STAND UP & BE COUNTED PILGRIM

John Wayne's
Pledge of Allegiance

I can well remember as a little boy standing up in my classroom every morning and reciting the Pledge of Allegiance. Shucks, I didn't know and I didn't care that the Pledge was first published in 1892 and that it was the result of a dream to have "a flag in every school." All I knew at the time was that for some doggone reason I had to hide my feelings from my classmates.

The inner excitement that came over me when I clasped my hand over my heart and said, "I pledge allegiance ..." was so great I just couldn't share it with anybody.

All that I knew then was that somehow, mysteriously, I belonged. I belonged to something far too profound for my young mind to comprehend. But, I belonged.

As I grew older, the mystery began to unfold. I wasn't just talking about some nebulous place a long way off, I was talking about the ground I was standing on. Ground that stretched from California to my Iowa homeland and beyond.

When I was five years old my parents moved from Winterset, Iowa, to Lancaster, California.

Imagine a five-year-old from the flat plains being plunked down in a land that had huge mountains looming over its western rim and more mountains that stretched for hundreds of miles eastward to the Mojave Desert. My horizons widened: so did my love, and yes, my awe of my country.

Now, after having traveled extensively throughout the world, every word of that Pledge is precious to me. For hidden in its simplicity there lies a tremendous power. Our republic stands for the innate dignity of all mankind, at the hideous cost of the Civil War.

We are one nation under God, indivisible: and ever since 1776 all the world is aware of our hunger for individual liberty and our thirst for justice.

The next time you say those words, let your mind wander back to those days when you stood in your classrooms and recited the Pledge of Allegiance. It was your first real commitment to your nation.

Your first real step to a bright new world.

— John Wayne

America, Why I Love Her. Lyrics by John Mitchum

INTRODUCTION

In his epic film, The Alamo, actor John Wayne's Davy Crockett says, *"Republic – I like the sound of the word. Republic is one of those words that makes me tight in the throat."*

That thought was also embedded in the heart and soul of Duke Wayne, the man. He loved the flag and what it stood for – especially the freedom and boundless opportunity visually represented by the American West with its magnificent eye-stretching horizons and breath-taking azure skies. It was a place where a man could take a deep breath and see clear into tomorrow.

It was a place where a man could take a

He knew that freedom was a dream to be cherished and nurtured constantly. When World War II was declared, he was married with four small children. It grieved him that he was over-age for the draft and had an injured shoulder that had cost him his football scholarship to the University of Southern California as well as his dream – an appointment to Annapolis Naval Academy.

But fate took Duke to the movies, and he rallied Americans around the flag by making films that portrayed our brave fighting men as the heroes they were, true patriots who laid their lives on the line for America, the land of the free and the home of the brave.

– Jane Pattie

deep breath and see clear into tomorrow.

I CAN WELL REMEMBER AS A LITTLE

every morning and reciting

Shucks, I DIDN'T KNOW AND

first published in 1892 and

BOY STANDING UP IN MY CLASSROOM

The Pledge of Allegiance.

I DIDN'T CARE THAT THE PLEDGE WAS

that it was the result of a dream

TO HAVE "A flag IN every SCHOOL."

Folks ... All of My Life

■ I've felt privileged to have good friends around me, privileged to have been able to do the kind of work I know and love the best, and to have been born in a country whose immense beauty and grandeur are only matched by the greatness of her people. ■ For a number of years I have tried to express a deep and profound love for these things: to be able to say what I feel in my heart. ■ I know most of you feel the same as I do about our country. Now and then we gripe about some of her imperfections but sometimes that's good, especially if it gets us working together to make things better. It seems to me we often take too much for granted and have a tendency to forget the good things about America. ■ My hope and prayer is that everyone knows and loves our country for what she really is and what she stands for. May we nurture her strengths and strengthen her weaknesses so that she will always be the land of the free and the home of the brave. ┘

– John Wayne

Jolu
WAYNE
IN
WESTWARD HO

DIRECTED BY
R.N. BRADBURY
PRESENTED BY
REPUBLIC PICTURES

STORY & SCREEN PLAY BY
ROBERT EMMETT
AND
LINDSLEY PARSONS

"Courage is being scared to death but saddling up anyway."   – John Wayne

"Once in a while, it's good to take note and find out what it is that you're taking pride in - is it worthwhile? Our free society has been terribly tampered with by bureaucracy. And as the society becomes less free, for some reason its virtues are weakened. The only way you can get that back is if each individual will take note of what he stands for."

– John Wayne

WAS THAT FOR SOME *doggone* REASON

FROM MY CLASSMATES.

"A man's
got to have
a code, a creed
to live by,
no matter
his job."

– John Wayne

AMERICAN

PRI

"Nobody ever saw a cowboy on the psychiatrist's couch."

– John Wayne

DE

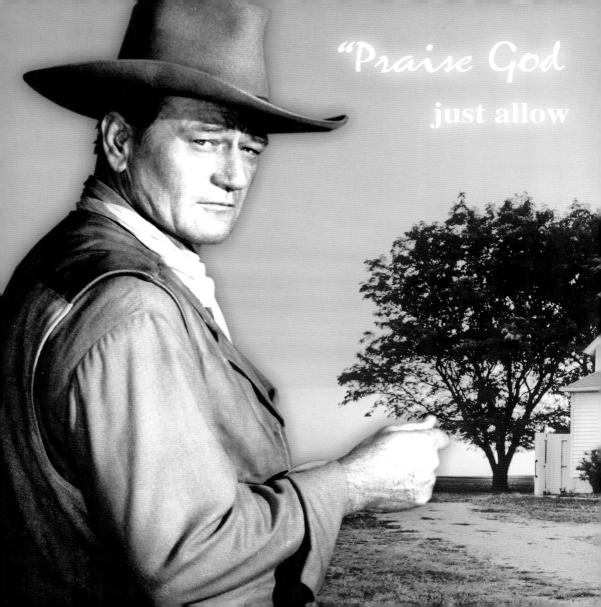

"Praise God

just allow

any way you so desire -
your neighbor the same right."

— John Wayne

The inner excitement

WHEN I CLASPED

AND SAID, "I Pledge

WAS so great I JUST COULDN'T

THAT CAME OVER ME
my hand OVER *my heart*

Allegiance ... "

SHARE IT WITH *anybody.*

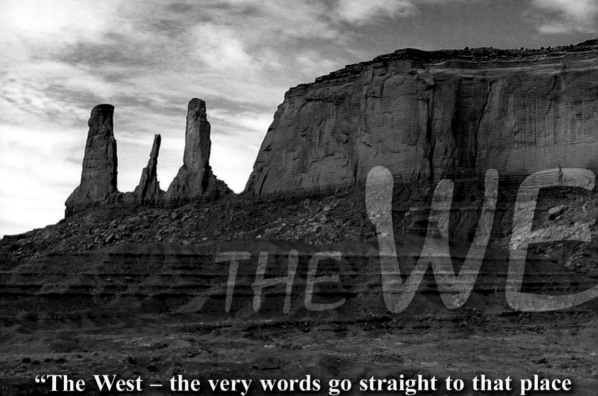

"The West – the very words go straight to that place of the heart where Americans feel the spirit of pride in their western heritage – the triumph of personal courage over any obstacle, whether nature or man."

– John Wayne

Duke, The Wonder Horse

"Planes, automobiles, trains – *they are great*, but when it comes to getting the audience's heart going, *they can't touch a horse.*"

– John Wayne –

ALL THAT I KNEW THEN *mysteriously,* I BELONGED TO *something young mind* TO COMPREHEND.

WAS THAT *somehow,*

I BELONGED.

FAR TOO PROFOUND FOR MY

BUT, *I Belonged.*

"We all have our disagreements – but let some other country step on our tail, and they'll find out how quickly Americans become united."

– John Wayne

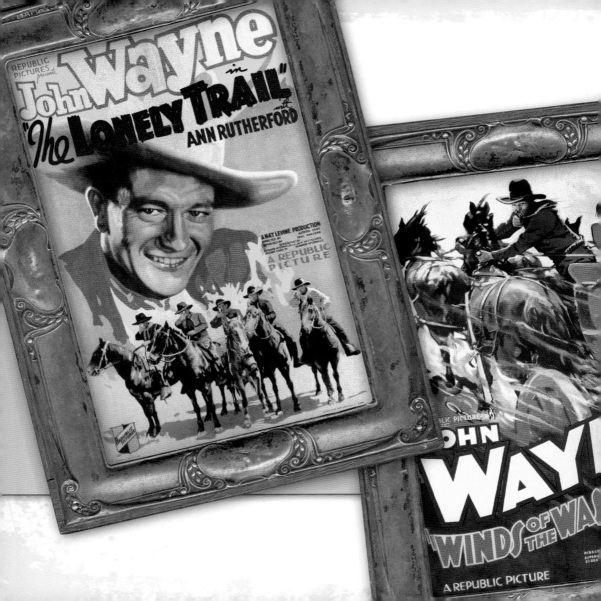

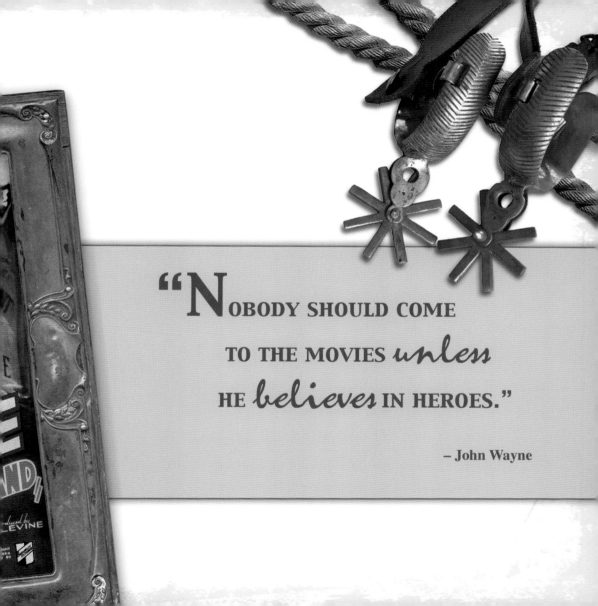

"**N**OBODY SHOULD COME
TO THE MOVIES *unless*
HE *believes* IN HEROES."

– John Wayne

As I grew older,

I WASN'T JUST TALKING ABOUT SOME

I was talking about the

GROUND THAT STRETCHED

MY IOWA HOMELAND

the mystery began to unfold.

NEBULOUS PLACE A LONG WAY OFF,

GROUND I WAS standing on.

FROM CALIFORNIA TO

and beyond.

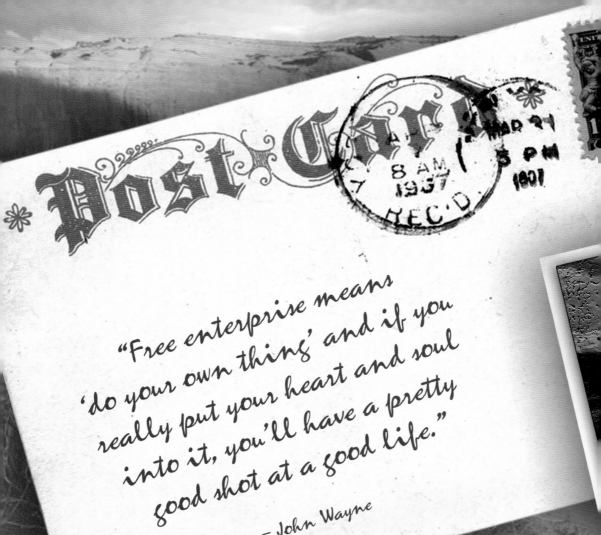

Post Card

MAR 24 8 AM 1937 REC'D · 3 PM 1801

"Free enterprise means 'do your own thing' and if you really put your heart and soul into it, you'll have a pretty good shot at a good life."

– John Wayne

"There's right and there's wrong — you gotta do one or the other. You do the one and you're living. You do the other and you may be walking round but in reality you're dead."

— John Wayne

When I was five years old

Imagine

A FIVE-YEAR-OLD FROM THE FLAT PLAINS

THAT HAD *huge* MOUNTAINS LOOMING

MOUNTAINS THAT STRETCHED

MY PARENTS MOVED FROM

WINTERSET, IOWA, TO LANCASTER, CALIFORNIA.

BEING PLUNKED DOWN IN A LAND

OVER ITS WESTERN RIM AND MORE

FOR *hundreds of miles*

EASTWARD TO THE MOJAVE DESERT.

John Wayne cast a long shadow
that stretched clear around the world.

He became a legend ...
a mixture of man, movie star and myth.

In real life he lived similar to J.B. Books's credo in *The Shootist.* "I won't be wronged. I won't be insulted. I won't be laid a hand on. I don't do these things to other people, and I require the same from them."

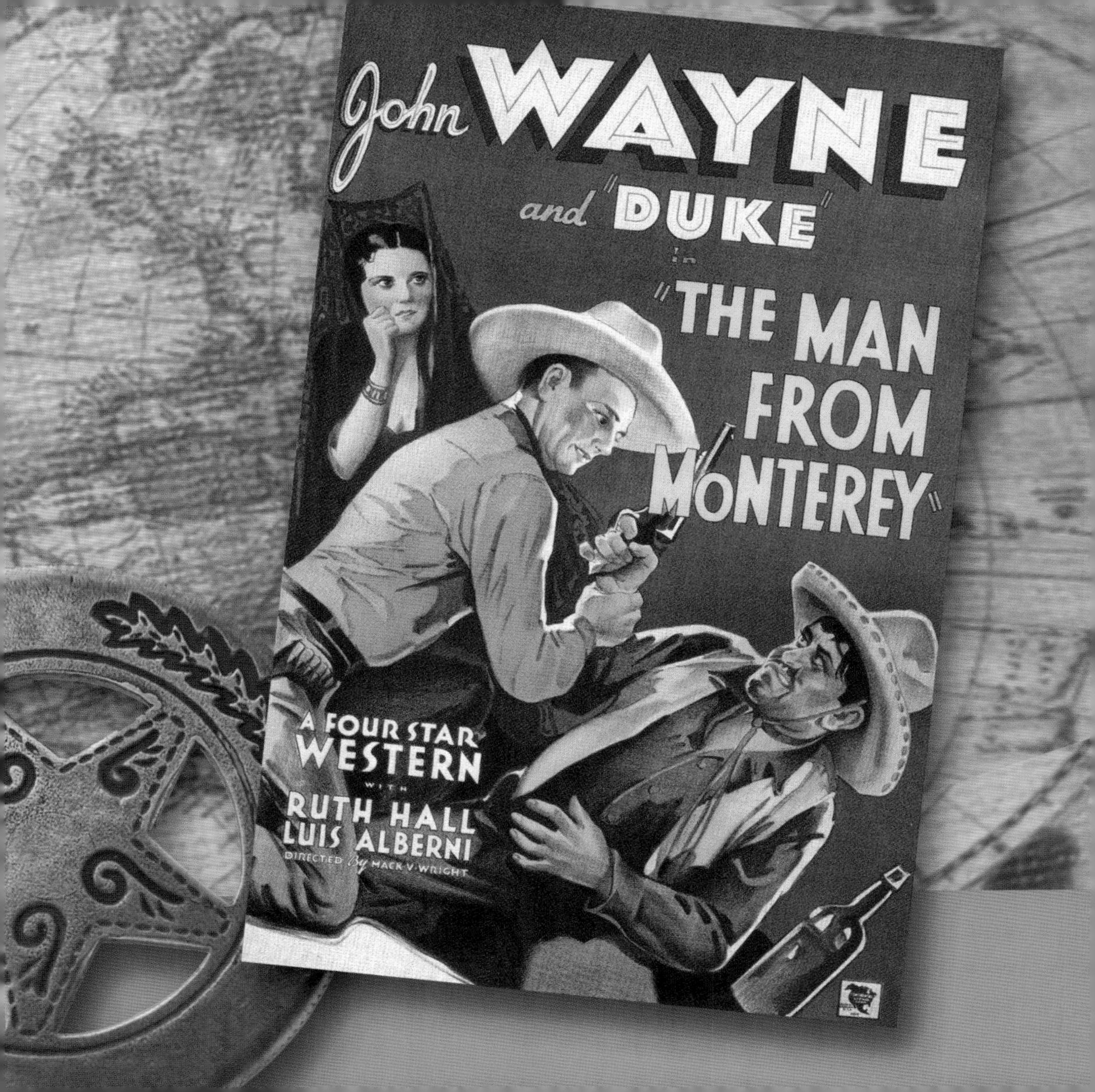
John WAYNE
and "DUKE"
in
"THE MAN FROM MONTEREY"
A FOUR STAR WESTERN
WITH
RUTH HALL
LUIS ALBERNI
DIRECTED By MACK V. WRIGHT

*Pictured: John Wayne
and Louis Johnson*

26 BAR RANCH

AN ENDURING PARTNERSHIP BETWEEN LIFE LONG FRIENDS

"I love this house and everybody in it!" Duke's voice boomed every time he exploded through the back door of the home of his most loyal friends, Louis and Alice Johnson, near Stanfield, Arizona. For two decades, both men had been partners in the cotton and cattle business since 1958 operating the Red River Land Company and the country's largest privately-owned computerized feedlot with a capacity of 90,000 head of cattle. The 50,000 acre 26 Bar Ranch near Springerville, Arizona, was home to their nationally famous purebred herd of award-winning Hereford cattle. Their annual bull sale each Fall saw buyers from across the country pay record-setting prices for the 26 Bar bloodlines. John Wayne once said that "Louie is one of the very few men I have truly trusted." In true Code of the West style, Duke and Louie were a proud American team.

MY HORIZONS
So did my love,

"When the road looks rough ahead, remember the *Man Upstairs* and the word *Hope*. Hang on to both and tough it out."

– John Wayne

"**W**hen you come slam bang up against trouble,
it never looks half as bad if you face up to it."

– John Wayne

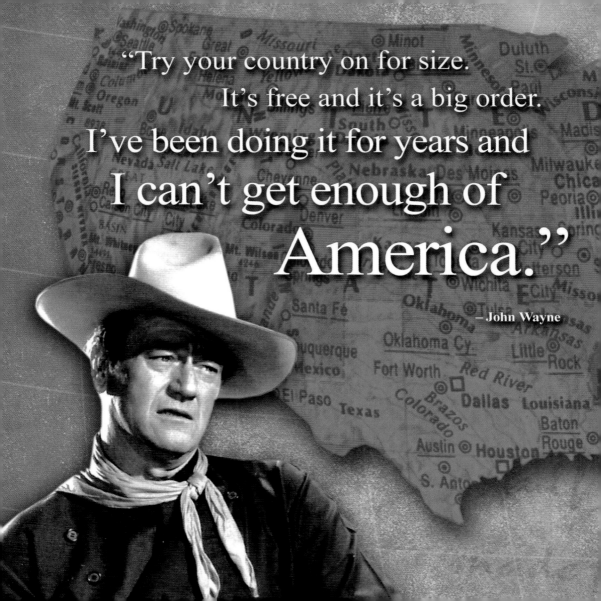

Now, AFTER HAVING

THROUGHOUT *the world*

PLEDGE IS

FOR HIDDEN IN ITS *simplicity*

OUR REPUBLIC *stands for* THE

AT THE *hideous cost*

TRAVELED EXTENSIVELY

every word OF THAT

PRECIOUS *to me.*

THERE LIES *a tremendous power.*

innate DIGNITY *of all mankind,*

OF THE CIVIL WAR.

DUKE

never forgot the advice of his father:

"Always keep your word;
a gentleman never insults
anyone intentionally; and
don't look for trouble, but
if you get into a fight, make
sure you win it."

Pictured: Father, Clyde Morrison with brother, Robert and "Little Duke" (Marion Morrison)

"... my heart cries out,

my pulse runs fast

at the might of her domain ...

You ask me why I love her?

I've a million reasons why:

My beautiful America,

Beneath God's wide, wide sky."

– John Wayne

America, Why I Love Her. Lyrics by John Mitchum

We are one NATION

AND EVER SINCE 1776 ALL THE

FOR *individual liberty*

"It's the parents' job to teach the child what his nation has done for him in the past and what it expects from him in the future."

– John Wayne –

Duke's Legacy

John Wayne's children: (Standing from left) Ethan, Melinda and Michael; (Sitting) Marisa, Aissa, Toni and Patrick.

JOHN WAYNE *loved life.*
He worked hard, played hard,
and lived every day to its fullest.

He never complained and he never explained.

Toward the end he said,
"I've had a great life. If I had a
chance to live it again, I wouldn't
change a thing." He had no regrets.
He was at peace. His spirit is truly
that of *the Great American West.*

The next time you say those words,

THOSE DAYS WHEN YOU STOOD

RECITED *The Pledge*

IT WAS *your* FIRST *real*

Your FIRST *real* STEP

let your mind wander back to

IN YOUR CLASSROOMS AND

of Allegiance.

COMMITMENT TO *your* NATION.

TO A BRIGHT *new world.*

— John Wayne

America, Why I Love Her. Lyrics by John Mitchum

The End

Web Site: www.TheDukeBook.com